The Salt and Sweet of Memory

Jenna Plewes

The Salt and Sweet of Memory

©Jenna Plewes

First Edition 2019

ISBN: 978-1-913329-05-1

Jenna Plewes has asserted her authorship and given her
permission to Dempsey & Windle for these poems to be
published here.

Published by Dempsey & Windle
15 Rosetrees
Guildford
Surrey
GU1 2HS
UK
01483 571164
dempseyandwindle.com

A CIP record for this book can be obtained from the British
Library.

Printed by CMP Ltd, Poole, Dorset, United Kingdom

Acknowledgements

Some of these poems have been published elsewhere: 'Yellow' was commended in the Ware Poets Competition 2019; 'Yellow' and 'Shaping a Pattern' were first published in *Orbis Magazine*; 'Queuing for Heaven' was commended in *Poetry on the Lake* competition and other poems have been published in *Reach* and *The Dawntreader*.

Previous collections by Jenna Plewes

Salt (Indigo Dreams Publishing 2013)
Pull of the Earth (Indigo Dreams Publishing 2016)
Against the Pull of Time (Pamphlet, V Press 2018)

Her poems have also been published in the *Rialto*, *Prole*, *Orbis*, *Artemis*, *The Cannon's Mouth*, *Sarasvati*, *The Dawntreader* and *Reach*.

The first poem in *Against the Pull of Time* was poem of the week on the Oxford Brookes poetry centre website in 2018).

She was highly commended in the Hastings International Competition in 2012, highly commended in the Geoff Stevens Memorial Prize in 2013 and 2014, commended in the Four Corners International Poetry Competition and in the Second Light Poetry Competition in 2015 and 2017. In 2016 and 2018 she was shortlisted in *Poetry on the Lake*, and *Poetry Space* competitions. She won 1st prize in the Settles Sessions Competition in 2017 and 3rd prize in the Barnet Poetry Competition in 2018, was runner up in the Settle Sessions competition 2018, won 2nd prize in Poetry Space competition 2019 and was runner-up in Ware Poets Competition 2019. In 2019 she was shortlisted in the Brian Dempsey Memorial Competition.

Contents

I

II

III

For Nigel and Adrian,
who know the best and the worst of me.

I

Army Overcoat

Did I flinch in the womb
when the sirens wailed?

I was born in the rattle of stones,
the clang of metal on metal.

My mother heaved me out
as the All Clear sounded.

Steeped in my blood
the salt and sweet of memory,

torchlight, dust and tweed,
banshee wail, and firecracker sparks.

I learnt to hold tight to your hand
when we ran.

My father reappeared when I was four,
big and loud, filling our little room.

Highland Haibun

It would have been our first Christmas in a highland croft in Stornaway, far away from the war. There would have been nappies drying on the high mesh fender and the smell of a smoky turf fire. There would have been women's soft gaelic voices, lullabies and songs. There's a sense of homecoming when I hear women singing in a certain way. The crying of gulls, the roar of wind and waves are memories before memory, but weren't there Christmas decorations that year, puffs of cotton wool threaded on long strings down the dark windows swaying in the draught as my mother came in from the cold, laughing?

long winter nights
Churchill on the home service
drifting in and out on a weak signal

Moving On

A troop train travels north
packed with sleeping men.
You were still breastfeeding,
fed me in the toilet,
smoked to hide the smell.

So many trains since then,
their sway and rumble
rain-smeared glass.

So many destinations,
departure and arrival times,
journeys I take, regret I cannot take.

So many days of packing and unpacking,
kitchen crockery, the standard lamp,
pictures wrapped in a bedside rug,

taking back one set of keys,
another set to fit into another door
another letterbox, another hall.

So many platforms, station stops,
keeping something precious
nested in an inside pocket
while the rails tick in the heat
and the tracks stretch out of sight.

The Box

(with apologies to Kit Wright)

Under my bed was a box

with the scream of a vixen tearing the dark,
a scritch-scratch of claws on the window-pane,
a creaking stair, and the click of a latch,
tip-tapping footsteps of rain.

Under my cot was a box

with curtains that moved in the draught,
a monstrous thing on the back of the door,
a worm of light that slid over the bed
and crawled off across the floor.

Under my bed was a box

with a lumpy pillow and tangled sheets,
whiskery fish that swam in the night
and the cry of a child for someone to come;
someone to turn on the light.

Elmer Sands 1947 – 49

Summer heat
tarmac blisters pimpling the lane,
our feet bark-brown
slaloming shingle banks,

concrete blocks, barbed wire tangles,
slip-weedy groynes, miles of rippled sand,
sea, safe and warm as bathwater.

Winter stormed our defences,
waves tore through wire,
fired shingle across the road,
soaked sandbag barricades,
left a carnage of dead and dying worms
on flooded lawns.

My father – briefcased, umbrella'd,
teetered on the garden wall
to keep his best shoes dry.

Little Brother

It sounded bad, thin bleating
cries cutting through jeering,
laughter, soft thuds.

I remember fighting
the huddle of bodies
kicking shins, hauling
the ringleader out by his hair,

picking up the broken NHS glasses,
wiping away snot and tears.

On the school bus home that night
the girl who'd never slammed a door
or stamped a foot

found bits of blond hair stuck
to her damp fist.

The Go-Between

'Our little ray of sunshine'
that's what you called me.

I kept the surface bright,
covered threadbare conversations,
hid broken promises
behind the cushions,

tried to mend the frayed rope
that held you both together
but the fibres had rotted
and when it finally broke
I was left holding the ends:

there was no slack left
to cobble them together.

Queuing for Heaven

We shuffle our way down the high street
snapping gaps shut against intruders,
letting friends push in beside friends.

Mike – late as usual – in a cloud of Old Spice,
elbows in beside Jen in new white boots,
blond beehive sparkling with spray.

We hunch against the wind, crane out,
Dave's got Annie – no sign of Bill,
they've split up again.

Our chatter dies as the door to paradise
opens. We watch the faces of those leaving,
see the fading shimmer of dreams.

Now the queue begins to move, the chosen
are ushered in. We, the unreserved, stand
in the rain, our fingers crossed.

Finally the blast of heat and light, a ticket
safe in a cold hand, wet coat under the seat,
a rustle of papery wings as the lights go down.

Questions without Answers

What did you think of me?
You never said – maybe I never heard.

Our family don't talk much.

I don't remember you in uniform,
they say I was sick in your cap
when you came home on leave.

Winding roads still make me ill.

Did I resent you
when you reappeared?

We went for family walks at Christmas,
found dead crows
pinned on a barbed wire fence.
You said they killed pheasant chicks,
gamekeepers left them as a warning
to other birds. You showed us the stars,
taught us the constellations.

As they grew up my brothers
helped you in your workshop,
learnt about veneers and dovetail joints.

Now when I'm stripping furniture
I wish I'd worked with you.

You often went away,
I guessed you had another life,
tiptoed round you.

What did you see in Mum?
She was young and pretty
went to the same church.
You found a badgers' sett
took her at night to see them.
You were a country boy,
had an egg round, she made jams,
sold them in the market.
You saved, married, had me.

In those early baby pictures
you look happy together.

War changed you,
we stayed the same.
Is that what happened?

You bought a London flat,
worked for the BBC
came home at weekends.

What were they like,
your London lovers?
I met the last —
the one you left us for,
cut her dead in Dingles.

She nursed you till the end,
I'm grateful now.

The day you left
I tried to talk to you.
You said it wasn't about me,
I wouldn't understand.
I held Mum while she cried.

Now when couples come to me
to mend or end relationships
I know it's seldom
what it seems.

I remember your charm,
how well you told a joke
how good you looked
your veneer impeccable –
how your body trembled as you
walked me up the aisle.

Your friends came to my wedding,
I don't remember many at the wake.

I never saw you cry,
we wrote each other letters,
never talked.
When you were dying I visited but kept
you at arms' length. I wasn't kind.

Mum kept your photo by her bed.
I took it when she died,
have it on my desk.

Handsome, successful,
were you lonely at the end?

I wish it had been different.
But I live with it,
bits of you like splinters still working
their way out.

What did you think of me?
You never said.

How much do tears weigh in a child's hands?

I bought your favourite chocolate
on my way home from school
wrapped it in little notes
begged you to eat.

You were beautiful,
thin as a blade of grass.

We played Scot Joplin
on the gramophone,
danced in the living room
but your eyes were sad.

What was the turning point?
Dad's leaving, or his death – years
later – in another woman's house.
I never asked, you never said.

Shadows lifted in your widowhood
you pleased yourself with what you wore
your sorrows made you wise.

You found your zany side again
easy to tease – pummelling your grown-up sons
till they bundled you high on the fridge
all five foot of you.

We had weekends away, the two of us.
I drove. You had the map. We found
green lanes, sat in tiny churches,
ate in country pubs, loved the same things.

You held the net, pulling in the shoal of us
each Christmas, helpless with laughter
at the same old jokes, same crazy games.

I wore red at your funeral.
we played 'The Entertainer' at the end.

Grief is a Journey without a Destination

You loved a force eight gale,
whitecaps and breaking spray,

I glimpsed the wildness in you once,
dancing in rain after drought,
alone and naked.

You gentled yourself to meet a husband's needs,
tore feathers from your breast
to keep us warm.

Too close to focus then, I only see it
clearly now.

A Stiff Bright Sleeve

Empty rooms have nothing to say,
a chest of drawers, conker-bright,
shines in the sunlight.

Drawers slide out like smiles,
sweaters, scarves, and gloves
and in the top drawer, tidied away,
your private things.

Clean white underwear,
Damart vests smelling of lavender,
a nest of coiled tights
like soft brown mice.

Wrapped in tissue paper at the back
the brooch I made when I was six
lopsided, smudged, put by
and never worn.

My brother's gift was better,
his always would be better,
a bruise I'd carried down the years
under a stiff bright sleeve.

No other jewellery, no other gifts
are left to find,
a small brooch in my hand
a soft kiss on my palm, no words.

Handfast

If I stretched out my arms
I could almost touch our house
with one hand, the sea
with the other, a running
jump across a strip of tarmac.

Over acres of summer holidays
my feet hardened to leather
raced across sand and shingle
scabs of tar picked off
by butter paper before I went to bed.

This little lane dips
its feet in the sea
blackberries taste of salt,
bluebells and bracken crowd
my walking stick.

Booted, I stand in the surf
reach out my arms
handfast to the sea.

II

Reading in Bed

Your heat thaws my frozen feet,
softens my body like wax
as I slide into sleep.

The only sounds

a moth hitting the lampshade,
rumble of the night train,
rustle of a turning page.

You're far beyond my reach.

I float out on the tide,
travel through swirling dream-waters
where you cannot go.

Held in the circle of the reading lamp
side by side we go our separate ways.

Poor Connection

Rain on the window, the signal falters, strengthens,
outside, a figure, head-torch bobbing, splashes past,
dog at his heels, smooth-coated, long-legged.
You're at your desk, in a pool of light, facing
a dark garden, rescue collie lying where the old dog lay
on the turn of the stair, where she can see the drive.
She's settling you say, comes to you for company,
places a paw on your knee, watches you write.
There are sheep in the field. You keep her on a lead,
walk her in the woods, take her with you to the pub.
You had a meal with friends; they sent their love.
You ask about my day, whether I'm warm enough.
Parallel lives, I hear it in your voice so much unsaid,
rain streams down the glass. The phone goes dead.

I could say so many things …

I could say you are 100 volts
zinging through me,
shocking me awake –

slow-breathing starlight,
warm hands, cold cheeks,
mulled wine and melting snow.

I could say you are blood beat,
rip-tide and rolling surf,
an ocean swell of longing,

frustrating as a jammed zip,
irritating as a half-remembered tune,
loving as a Border Collie.

I could say you are bedtime stories,
tents and sleeping bags, pushchairs
and sensible family cars,

comfortable as well-worn walking boots,
reliable as an Ordnance Survey map,
faithful as firelight.

I could say you are honeysuckle
wound round my heart, bedded
deep in my being.

Shedding

Through the window
I watch leaves make their final landing,
settle on the lawn,
a foxy blanket shaken by the wind
flung on the ground.

Behind me is a lifeless room,
bare shelves, empty curtain poles,
dust sheets covering the floor.

Exercise books and mouldy paperbacks
lie in untidy heaps,
lego men, their faces horribly disfigured by hungry mice
lie decently buried in plastic bags.

A limp-eared, one-eyed bear
clings to life,
a rubic cube, a fishing rod, a box marked 'private'
packed up and labelled 'keep'.

As the sky darkens
mirrored in the glass
I see a naked light bulb
shine like a moon
in the stripped trees,

it is time to go.

III

Cuttings

Thin wands of new beginnings,
four rose cuttings to a pot

each one a pencil writing in darkness,
a thought earthed before sleep,

liminal, elusive, language
rooted in its loam.

Ideas pushing, pushing upwards,
words unfolding like leaves.

Home

A settling, a warmth, a smell of safety,
something from before there were words,
a lulling in the wind, a patterning of light,

a resting place and then a moving on.

Interlude

On this day the air is still, aspen leaves
shift and spin, then droop in the heat.

Two buzzards are peeling the sky like an apple,
an easy unwinding, spiral by spiral.

The river is illusive in its stillness. Twinned in the water,
willow-herb and tall bleached grasses waver as a swan
powers past

muscling the surface. The current mouths my hand,
milking my fingers, ungloving me.

On this day while insects whir and crawl, bees forage
and butterflies jig, a painted lady lands on a butterbur leaf,

opens her glorious tapestry and rests beside me, motionless.

Summer Solstice

Swallows are hunting
the heavens,
hour after hour
looping and diving
arrowing into the eaves.

Fledglings fluster
in an open-mouthed
frenzy for food,
driving them on.

Daylight drains away,
the crowded nest is quiet.
There's star-shine in the grass,
the bright beacons of glow-worms
guiding their lovers in.

A few short hours before
another dawn, the moon's
full-term, ripe as a melon.

You sleep beside me
curled on your side as always.
The swallows sleep
and glow-worms shine
their steady lights.

Chance Meeting

The splashing jolted me out of a daydream,
took me to the stream,

three wet-rug heads, unmoving,
huge liquid eyes, unblinking,
unafraid.

Three full-grown otters,
larger than large,
slick-furred in the clear shallows under the bridge,
gifted their gaze
then turned in formation back into shadow.

Faces from a greener world
tipped towards me; making
a connection,   or reconnection?

then a falling away   a fading
into ordinary time.

A Summer Day

heat hammers walls, roofs, streets,
cicadas buzz high in the branches,
thicken the air with endless tinnitus.

In the park children play in a skin of water,
a woman strolls with a kitten on a lead,
it lunges at a pigeon, patters on beside her.

Leaves are a pointillist pattern against the sky,
a breeze shifts ripples of light, pollen dusts
the surface of the pond, the children's hair.

It is one of those slow days, when nothing
much happens, that drip like resin,
trapping each tiny detail in amber.

Yellow

1

It was the last colour to go; the brightness she could still
see. I picked daffodils for her room, grew a Graham
Thomas rose, took her the buds so she could see them
open, smell the scent. I picked the last one today.

2

The candle flame is almost still, just a quiver when I turn
a page, a bright sheath around a shadowed core that's
sometimes blue, sometimes almost brown – the wick's
black finger-bone, a hook to catch another thought.

3

I wonder what he thought when the plough spat out that
first speck of gold and he wiped off the mud. I stare at
mangled twists of filigree in a glass case, marvel at their
intricate beauty; how fifteen centuries have passed since
an unknown goldsmith set garnets from Sri Lanka in a
jewelled hilt.

4

They are fierce and wild, those blazing yellow eyes. This
hawk glares through the bars, grips a worn perch with
huge, curved talons. He should be surfing the sky, reading
the wind, pinions quivering as he circles the thermals, not
one more prisoner longing for light and wind and rain.

5

I'm sitting in the sun, wearing my favourite skirt, the
colour of a crocus throat – and they come, a bumblebee
and then another, a dusting of tiny insects, and then the
butterflies, a painted lady and a monarch. They settle in
the folds of cotton, open a window into their world. If I
had closed my eyes against the light, they could have
come and gone and I would never know.

6

Waiting in the front pew it comes back to me after all
these years; the bowl of brown eggs on the larder shelf,
the cup with blue and white bands. I'm holding the egg,
tapping it just hard enough to make a crack. Then comes
the careful opening, the slip and slop of the yolk from
shell-dimple to shell-dimple, sliding the shiny yellow ball
into the cup. Granny's smile when I got it right, how it lit
up the room.

Walking into another Life

snow on the tops
a valley in shadow
a river in spate
uneven, stony paths
church
wind-voices in pines
nursery rhymes
waymarks on rocks
lichen
a fallen fingerpost

grey dust in empty rooms
blackened walls
a millwheel in the long grass
sheep droppings in the

a torn map, a book of

headstones scabbed with

butterflies on buddleia

Forged from Ice and Fire

Dragon bones picked clean by centuries
of grinding ice, splintered by frost,
gnawed by gale force winds.

Sheep-shelter niches snagged with wool.
Hazel Tor, Vixen Tor, Ausewell Rocks,
Allerbrook Outcrop, Bag Tor and Bee Tor,

Summer scrambling, tip-balanced building blocks,
skew-wiff in a sea of bee-buzzing, lark-loud heather,
Bowerman's Nose, Chat Tor and Cater's Beam,

strange, silvery creatures forged from ice and fire
their granite finger bones and vertebrae
way-marking the heaving oceans of the moor.

Banishing the Dark

The branch was perfect
                antlered, lichen-crusted
sprayed silver
                anchored in a pot

weighted with stones
                it stood in the window

necklaced with tinsel and trinkets
                tree lights wound around its bones

and when it was done, a hundred fireflies
                settled on its twigs

shone on silver birds, bells, and strings of beads
                when it grew dark

the silver tree found its twin in the black window
                beckoned it into the light

back to back through long winter nights they keep watch
                while the wild hunt skirls in the wind and rain.

Hoar Frost

Come outside with me, where
the cold will whip you awake,

walk in the winter woods while
they're cobwebbed and white,

see how each twig, each scalloped
holly leaf is furred with frost.

Above our heads a waterfall of catkins
gold against blue,

each breath blurs the future,
each step leaves its print.

Sunlight warms minute after minute,
sliding them through our mittened hands.

Shaping a Pattern

They were like seals –
        boulders she bedded
                in the dry garden

smooth, bulging bladders
            shining with wet

slow journeys
        ankle deep in a
              beer-brown stream

its cool splash and drag
          against her legs

light-shimmering on water
        ripple-shadow on
              river- rounded
stones
voluptuous,
        hand-heavy

a careful choosing,
         lifting
           mud-slippery

clink of pebbles in the pail
            a long, arm-aching
wandering back

meticulous placing
           one by one in its
                      scrape of shingle.

It occupied her mind,
rinsed her soul,
for a few hours she was happy.

Valdes lay
on the other side of the world,
its seals asleep on the shore,
held in the pendulum swing of
                the tides,
                    the days,
                      the years.

Untamed

Despite its tranquil surface show
the sea is treacherous,
cannot be trusted.
Under its smiling summer face
a rip-tide waits for swimmers
who venture out too far, carries them beyond the bay
drowning their cries.

It tempts with water warm as silk,
gentling cats-paws stroking skin,
but beware
the sea's a wildcat,
keep away when she unsheathes her claws.

The Truth, the Whole Truth and
Nothing but the Truth

Lark-song, heat and high ground, cloud-hair streaming
in a westerly wind, winter wheat rippling like the sea.

In one field a gush of poppies haemorrhages, I kneel
for a dramatic shot, one bloom, up close: pleated silk
with shadowy depths, spiderlings in a pool of blood.

Dust and dry earth, the prickle of a nettle sting, bees
buzzing somewhere out of sight, poppies swaying.

Bottle the sunlight, the last tepid swig from the flask,
the blister on my right heel, the dog's pricked ears,
pendulum-swing of her tail, the powder-print of our feet.

Will a poem trap the essence of this day? Each word, each phrase
floats free, settling, seeding where it lands.

Your memories will not be mine, the ones we share will blur.
We'll delete the inconvenient, highlight and filter, manipulate
the facts and still the larks will sing, poppies flood the fields.

In Memory of

No one sits here now.
The wood has weathered,
colour softened to old silver.

Lichen stitches crusty circles along the arms,
fallen leaves bunch underneath. Bird droppings whiten.
A breeze ruffles the tall grasses, seed-heads sway, bees hum.

Clouds drift, shadows come and go. Sunlight
eases itself along the seat, leans back, stretches out
a long finger to trace, one by one, the words I know by heart.